The Queen's Mirror

Written by Lisa Thompson
Pictures by Andy Hamilton

The Queen had a magic mirror.

It was very good at finding things.

The Princess lost her tiara, and she looked and looked for it.

The mirror knew exactly where it was.

"Look under your bed," it said.

"I can't find my dragon," said the Prince.

The mirror knew exactly where it was.

"Look at the top of the tower," said the mirror.

"Where is my sword?" said the Knight.

The mirror knew exactly where it was.

"Swim to the bottom of the moat," said the mirror.

"My mixing spoon has gone," said the Cook.

The mirror knew exactly where it was.

"Have you looked behind the big barrels?" said the mirror.

The Queen could not find the King.

And the Queen could not find the mirror either!

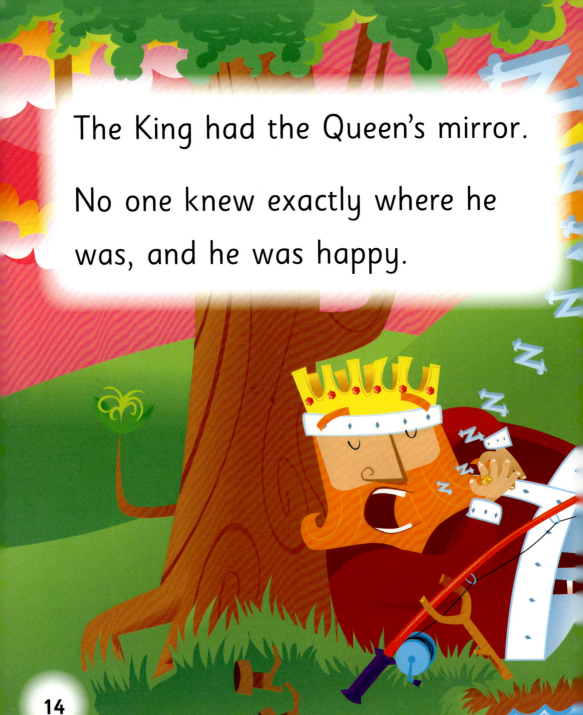

The King had the Queen's mirror.

No one knew exactly where he was, and he was happy.